Frisky was a little lamb.

She lived in a farmyard with a cat,

a horse, three ducks and six hens.

Frisky was always getting up to mischief.

One day Frisky wanted to play with

the cat.

But the cat was fast asleep on the wall.

Frisky ran up to the cat.
'I want to play,' said Frisky.

'Zzzz,' said the cat.

Frisky jumped on to the wall.
'I want to play,' said Frisky.

'But I don't want to play,'
said the cat.

The cat ran in to the shed.
Frisky ran in to the shed too.

'I want to play,' said Frisky.
'But I don't want to play.
I want to sleep,' said the cat.

The cat ran to the tree.
Frisky ran to the tree too.

The cat jumped in to the tree.
'I can sleep now,' said the cat.

'But I want to play now!'
said Frisky.

Frisky jumped in to the tree.

'Help!' said Frisky.
'Help!' said the cat.